YOUR KNOWLEDGE HAS VALUE

- We will publish your bachelor's and master's thesis, essays and papers

- Your own eBook and book - sold worldwide in all relevant shops

- Earn money with each sale

Upload your text at www.GRIN.com
and publish for free

Bibliographic information published by the German National Library:

The German National Library lists this publication in the National Bibliography; detailed bibliographic data are available on the Internet at http://dnb.dnb.de .

This book is copyright material and must not be copied, reproduced, transferred, distributed, leased, licensed or publicly performed or used in any way except as specifically permitted in writing by the publishers, as allowed under the terms and conditions under which it was purchased or as strictly permitted by applicable copyright law. Any unauthorized distribution or use of this text may be a direct infringement of the author s and publisher s rights and those responsible may be liable in law accordingly.

Imprint:

Copyright © 2018 GRIN Verlag
Print and binding: Books on Demand GmbH, Norderstedt Germany
ISBN: 9783668666115

This book at GRIN:

https://www.grin.com/document/417210

David Schneider

Which, if any, meta-ethical view do you find most compelling for the purposes of political theory?

GRIN Verlag

GRIN - Your knowledge has value

Since its foundation in 1998, GRIN has specialized in publishing academic texts by students, college teachers and other academics as e-book and printed book. The website www.grin.com is an ideal platform for presenting term papers, final papers, scientific essays, dissertations and specialist books.

Visit us on the internet:

http://www.grin.com/

http://www.facebook.com/grincom

http://www.twitter.com/grin_com

Which, if any, meta-ethical view do you find most compelling for the purposes of political theory?

3073 words

Meta-ethics, the study of the ontological foundations of ethics (Sayre-McCord 2012), is one of the big topics for moral and political philosophy. In this essay I argue that conventional constructivism (conventionalism) is the most compelling meta-ethical view for the purposes of political theory. First, (i) I determine what the purposes of political theory are. Then, (ii) I define logical validity and the ability to accommodate pluralism as requirements that a meta-ethical view must fulfil to be compelling for the purposes of political theory. Since conventional constructivism is a cognitivist, minimal realist and non-objectivist view (Bagnoli 2017), I show that a) cognitivism is logically valid, b) minimal realism is reasonably preferable to error theory and c) full-blown realism, opposed to non-objectivism, doesn't fulfil the requirement of validity. I provide examples which illustrate that this applies also to virtual reality ("VR"). Based on a)–c), I argue that d) non-objectivist conventional constructivism fulfils both the *validity* and the *pluralism requirement* for a meta-ethical view to be compelling for the purposes of political theory. I support this with what I call *the wake-up argument*.

(i) **The purposes of political theory**

The purpose of political theory is to address "conceptual, normative, and evaluative questions concerning politics and society, broadly construed. Examples are: When is a society just? What does it mean for its members to be free? When is one distribution of goods socially preferable to another?" (List and Valentini 2017, 525). Given space constraints, I focus in this essay on *analytic* political theory, the core branch of contemporary political theory (ibid.). Analytic political theory is "typically associated with certain features, such as clarity, systematic rigour, narrowness of focus, and an emphasis on the importance of reason." (McDermott 2008, 11).

(ii) **Requirements for a compelling meta-ethical view for the purposes of political theory**

A compelling meta-ethical view for the purposes of *analytic* political theory must be in accordance with the 'scientific' nature of analytic political theory. That is, it must be grounded on logically valid arguments. Call this the *validity requirement*. Besides, compelling meta-ethical view for the purposes of (analytic) political theory must be able to account for the fact that there is – due to a pluralism of ideas, people(s) and cultures – no single right answer to the questions that political theory addresses. Call this the *pluralism requirement*.

a) Cognitivism is logically valid

Cognitivists (conventional constructivists being part of them) hold that moral claims such as 'torturing children is wrong' purport to report facts (Van Roojen 2013). This is plausible, because we talk and reason about moral matters in ways similar to how we talk and reason about ordinary factual matters:

if, as the cognitivists suggest, moral claims resemble ordinary beliefs about the world, these moral claims are (analogous to ordinary factual beliefs) also apt for truth and falsity (DeLapp). For example, people, when asked on the street, wouldn't be hesitant to confirm that they believe the moral claim 'torturing children is wrong' to be true. Beyond treating moral claims - like empirical facts - as true or false, it becomes evident that we talk and reason about moral matters in ways similar to how we talk and reason about empirical matters when comparing an argument that involves moral claims (argument 1) with an argument that involves ordinary empirical claims (argument 2) (ibid.):

Argument 1:

P1: Torturing children is wrong

P2: Sophie is a child

C: Therefore torturing Sophie is wrong

Argument 2:

P1: All humans are mortal

P2: Socrates is a human

C: Therefore Socrates is mortal

In both arguments prevails the same reasoning pattern (the so-called syllogism) - true premises lead to a true conclusion. This suggests some kind of parity in the cognitive status of those claims. In case cognitivism was not true (moral claims expressing something other than truth-apt propositions) then it would not be clear 1) why we are nevertheless able to deduce a conclusion from moral sentences or 2) how we would otherwise define validity. Consequently, since we appear to be able to legitimately apply the syllogism in argument 1, moral claims must be truth-apt. This approach to defend cognitivism is known as the Frege-Geach Problem which cannot be outlined more in detail in this essay (for a more comprehensive discussion, see Geach 1965 and Schueler 1988).

Not only in the Real World, but also in VR we talk and reason about moral matters in ways similar to how we talk and reason about empirical matters. The fact of being in VR doesn't put an end to forming (moral) arguments from premises to conclusions. Therefore, in VR one also purports to report facts when expressing moral claims.

Even if these arguments in favour of cognitivism are convincing, there remains a challenge for cognitivists, namely Michael Smith's moral problem. Smith argues that there is a tension between three intuitively plausible meta-ethical doctrines (one of them being cognitivism). At most two of the following three claims can be true (Smith 1994, 12f):

I. Moral judgments are beliefs, not desires or emotions (Cognitivism)

II. Moral judgments are intrinsically motivating (Internalism)

III. Both beliefs and desires are necessary for motivation (The Humean thesis about motivation)

To sustain cognitivism, either internalism or the humean thesis about motivation must be proved false. Either of the two views can be proved false by delivering convincing arguments for the respective other view. The following illustrations provides good reasons to believe that the humean thesis about motivation is true (and internalism false): a belief *b* like 'there is a unique pastry in the bakery around the corner' is (alone) not enough to motivate a person *p* who holds this belief to go and get this pastry if she doesn't care about this pastry. To be motivated to go and get the pastry, a person *p* needs in addition to her belief *b* a desire *d*. Analogously, the belief 'torturing children is wrong' must be accompanied by a desire to be moral in order to motivate a person to not torture children. Consequently, the Humean thesis about motivation is valid and internalism is false. This solves Smith's moral problem and ensures that cognitivism can be sustained.

In VR, motivation works (in human avatars)[1] in the same way as in the RW. Merely holding a belief does also not lead in VR to an action if it is not accompanied by a desire to realise that belief. In VR, to turn moral beliefs into motivation, the role of the desire of being moral might even be more important than in the RW: suppose, one holds the belief 'torturing children is wrong' and one knows that torturing AI-driven child avatars (that don't represent a real human being but are completely artificial) in VR doesn't harm any real child. In this case it might still be immoral to torture the AI-child in VR – immoral in the same way as it would be to have a Hakenkreuz flag hanging in your private bedroom without harming anyone. But since no direct harm towards a child is involved,[2] the desire to be moral might have to be higher than in cases of direct harm to be motivated not to torture the AI-driven child in VR.

b) Minimal realism is reasonably preferable to error theory

After having shown why it is compelling to believe that moral claims purport to report facts, the question is whether there exist truly such facts – which would lead to (at least minimal) realism (of which conventional constructivism is part) – or not – which would be an indicator for the error theory (Sayre-McCord 1986, 6f). Error theorists argue that we talk as if there were moral facts, but there aren't any: when a person makes a moral claim or engages in moral discourse, this person tries to report facts and express beliefs much like ordinary factual beliefs, but she is systematically mistaken and deluded, the moral facts to which she purports to report are only an illusion (Lillehammer 2004, 95f). This challenge to (at least minimal) realism is not convincing, because it seems to go against Davidson's principle of charity in interpreting people: the thought that the entire practice of moral discourse is mistaken in its globality is an uncharitable way of interpreting human practices, **unless we have very**

---

[1] Given space constraints, questions regarding motivation and agency of person-like beings in VR that are powered by computational power and algorithms cannot be discussed in this paper.

[2] Indirect forms of harm for real children could be that the threshold of torturing real children gets lowered by torturing AI-driven child avatars. See for example: Buckingham, Angela. 2016. "Murder in VR Should Be Illegal." Vice Motherboard. https://motherboard.vice.com/en_us/article/aekaxk/should-murder-in-vr-be-illegal. Torturing child avatars in VR (representations of real children), of course, leads to a direct psychological harm for children.

strong evidence for it – or no better (i.e. more charitable) interpretation is available (Davidson 1991, 158). Since we don't have very good evidence for this and there is a more charitable interpretation available - (at least minimal) realism - it is reasonable to reject the error theory in favour of (at least minimal) realism.

c) Full-blown realism, opposed to non-objectivism, doesn't fulfil the requirement of validity

Good arguments for the denial of (i) moral non-cognitivism and (ii) moral error theory show that (at least minimal) moral realism, of which conventional constructivism is part of, is in accordance with the *requirement of validity*. A minimal realist conceives the moral facts as genuinely existent. Specifying these truly existent moral facts further regarding whether they are mind/subject-dependent or not leads to either full-blown realism (moral facts are mind/subject independent) or non-objectivism (moral facts are mind/subject dependent) (Joyce 2015). Since conventional constructivism is a kind of non-objectivism, I show in the following first that full-blown moral realism doesn't fulfil the requirement of validity. Based on this, I will then show that that conventional constructivism fulfils both requirements for a meta-ethical view to be compelling for the purposes of political theory.

Full-blown realism can be divided in two sorts: *naturalistic* realism and *non-naturalistic* realism. Both sorts fail to fulfil the validity requirement. *Naturalistic* realism conceives moral facts as being 'natural' (or as being supervened on natural facts) (Sayre-McCord 2015). It should be possible to derive certain 'ought' facts from these natural facts. But this is logically impossible, since natural facts are 'is' facts and, according to G. E. Moore, one cannot derive an 'ought' from an 'is.' (Moore 1903, § 10 and § 13). *Non-naturalistic* realism conceives moral facts as being distinct from natural facts (and as not being supervened on them) (Sayre-McCord 2015). Since the natural world is causally closed, it is logically impossible that we could ever learn about these facts, since we could not causally interact with them. Even if the rules of causality constructed for VR differed partially from those of the RW, the constructed VR-rules of causality still wouldn't enable humans in VR to interact with non-naturalistic moral facts, because they also would be outside of the causally closed virtual world.

d) Non-objectivist conventional constructivism fulfils the *validity* <u>and</u> the *pluralism requirement*

Constructivism, a sort of non-objectivism, provides a non-mysterious, logically valid, account of conceiving moral facts by saying that moral facts are facts that we as individuals, or as a society, or as humanity, or as rational beings construct explicitly ourselves (Joyce 2015). The moral facts are constituted, according to constructivism, by what agents would agree to in an idealized process of rational deliberation, choice, or agreement (Bagnoli 2017). In conventionalism, a form of constructivism, this idealized process of constituting moral facts is not constrained by universal features of practical reason (I do not deny that there are certain minimally universal patterns of human cognition), but by (social) conventions that (can) differ between groups within specific traditions

(Wong 2008, 265). Since the truth of moral claims is relative to specific groups or practices, conventionalist constructivism is thus a form of relativism (Harman 1975, 3).

Critics of conventional constructivism could argue that if moral facts are just facts that you or your community have somehow constructed, then it is hard to interpret disagreements across different communities as genuine disagreements. Conventional constructivists could counter that, indeed, there is a disagreement between communities, namely a disagreement regarding which moral beliefs communities with despairing moral beliefs should agree on as standard for their interactions. Due to certain minimally universal patterns of human cognition, different communities can end up constructing similar moral beliefs. Furthermore, if we consider that law, for example, is socially constructed, the idea that there is such a thing as morality or normativity which doesn't involve any act of human construction seems implausible. Having hereby proven that conventional constructivism fulfils the *requirement of validity*, consider now *the wake-up argument* as a proof that it also fulfils the *requirement of pluralism*:

Sally has spent all her conscious living time in VR, her physical body gets fed and taken care of automatically, without her conscious effort. Through her socialisation in VR, she has built up (i.e. constructed) her moral views in VR. She has always known about the existence of the so called Real World, but has no detailed knowledge about it. She has always had the desire to find out what it is like to be living in the Real World. To satisfy her curiosity, she one day decides to 'wake up' and to leave VR. When living in the RW:

1) Some of her virtual moral beliefs hold true/are similar to the moral beliefs she encounters in the RW.

For instance, what the people who spend most of their living time in the RW (and occasionally immerse into VR) coined as the belief 'torturing children (including AI child-avatars) in VR is wrong' meant for her simply 'torturing children is wrong.' Since she spent her whole life in the VR, a) she hadn't learnt how to distinguish between AI-driven children and human child avatars rendering the extension 'including AI child-avatars' obsolete for her and b) the local specification 'in VR' is obsolete for her; VR was her usual frame of reference.

2) Some of her moral beliefs remain in principle the same but require some adaptation to her new environment.

For instance, the moral belief 'judging people for their physical appearance is wrong' must be redefined from 'Judging people for the avatar they choose is wrong' (in VR) to 'Judging people for the skin colour that nature gave them is wrong.'

3) Some of her moral beliefs become obsolete.

For example, 'torturing AI-driven avatars is wrong,' assuming that there are no AI-driven avatars in the RW. Of course, due to hologram and augmented reality technology, there might one day be AI-driven avatars that seem as realistically in the RW as in VR. In this case this moral belief wouldn't be obsolete, for the same reasons as to why it would be wrong to torture AI-driven child avatars outlined at the end of section a).

4) She must construct some entirely new moral beliefs.
As the biological bodies behind the human avatars in VR are automatically nourished in the RW without a conscious effort by the body's owner, the topic of nutrition is not present in VR. Therefore, Sally has never been confronted with the possibility of a lack of food prior to leaving VR. Thus, she hasn't developed any moral beliefs regarding just food distribution in case of famine. When living in one of the two remaining human settlements whose inhabitants spend most of their living-time in the RW, she learns about the moral beliefs 'in case of famine, sharing food equally among all inhabitants is wrong' and 'men should receive more food than women in case of famine.' The reason for this, she has been told, is the inhabitant's communal conception of personhood: female inhabitants of this colony would be happy to starve in case of famine, knowing that the additional food would give their men the energy necessary to successfully perform dangerous tasks that require a high physical strength, such as repairing greenhouses on the surface of Mars. This would ensure the provision of new food which would lead to the survival of the whole group.

If Sally would have chosen to live with the other remaining VR-abstinent human settlement (which is situated on Earth and not on Mars), she would have developed different moral beliefs regarding just food distribution. An unequal distribution of the remaining food in case of famine would there be seen – because of the individual conception of personhood that underlies this colony – as highly unfair. A possible moral belief regarding just food distribution could be, for instance, 'everyone gets an equal share of the remaining food.' (For a detailed account of the distinction between communal and individual conception of personhood, see Flikschuh 2016).

The sections 2), 3) and 4) of this thought experiment show that the construction of a pluralism of moral beliefs is constrained by (social) conventions that (can) differ between groups within specific traditions. Since this is in accordance with conventional constructivists' notion that the truth of moral claims is relative to specific groups or practices, conventionalist constructivism fulfils the *pluralism requirement*. (In addition to that, the wake-up argument is – taken that it is valid – another proof that conventional constructivism fulfils the *requirement of validity*.)

Conclusion

There are two contingencies of the argument I made in this essay: first, I didn't evaluate *all* meta-ethical views, only the most prominent ones; second, the requirements for a meta-ethical view to be compelling could be different for non-analytic approaches to political theory such as continental, Eastern and African political philosophy. Yet, I argued in this essay that, in the proposed framework, we have good reasons to think that conventional constructivism is the most compelling meta-ethical view for the purposes of political theory. Since conventional constructivism is a cognitivist, minimal realist and non-objectivist view, I showed that cognitivism is logically valid, that minimal realism is reasonably preferable to error theory and that full-blown realism – opposed to non-objectivism – doesn't fulfil the requirement of validity. Based on this, I argued that non-objectivist conventional constructivism fulfils both the *validity* and the *pluralism requirement*. I supported this with *the wake-up argument*. Based on *the wake-up argument* and previous examples considering VR, I conclude that conventional constructivism is also the most compelling meta-ethical view for the political theorisation of VR. Thereby, I provide a first step towards the beginning of a debate around the formulation of the meta-ethics of VR, a debate that is highly relevant for the emerging field 'Political Philosophy of Virtual Reality.'

Bibliography

Bagnoli, Carla. 2017. "Constructivism in Metaethics." In *The Stanford Encyclopedia of Philosophy*, edited by Edward N. Zalta. https://plato.stanford.edu/entries/constructivism-metaethics/.

Buckingham, Angela. 2016. "Murder in VR Should Be Illegal." Vice Motherboard. https://motherboard.vice.com/en_us/article/aekaxk/should-murder-in-vr-be-illegal.

Davidson, Donald. 1991. "Three Varieties of Knowledge." In *Royal Inititute of Philosophy Supplement* 30, p. 153-166.

DeLapp, Kevin M. "Metaethics." In *The Internet Encyclopedia of Philosophy*, edited by James Fieser and Bradley Dowden. http://www.iep.utm.edu/metaethi/#SH3a.

Flikschuh, Katrin. 2016. "The arc of personhood: Menkiti and Kant on becoming and being a person." In *Journal of the American Philosophical Association* 2 (3), p. 437-455.

Geach, Peter. 1965. "Assertion." In *Philosophical Review* 74, p. 449-465.

Harman, Gilbert. 1975. "Moral Relativism Defended." In *Philosophical Review* 84(1), p. 3–22.

Joyce, Richard. 2015. "Moral Anti-Realism." *Stanford Encyclopedia of Philosophy,* edited by Edward N. Zalta, Fall 2015. https://plato.stanford.edu/archives/fall2015/entries/moral-anti-realism/.

Lillehammer, Hallvard. 2004. "Moral error theory." In *Proceedings of the Aristotelian Society*, 104, p. 93–109.

List, Christian/Valentini, Laura. 2016. "The Methodology of Political Theory." In *Oxford Handbook of Philosophical Methodology*, edited by Herman Cappelen, Tamar Szabó Gendler and John Hawthorne. Oxford: Oxford University Press.

McDermott, Daniel. 2008. "Analytical political philosophy." In *Political theory: methods and approaches*, edited by David Leopold and Marc Stears. Oxford: Oxford University Press.

Moore, G. E. 1903. "Principia Ethica." Cambridge: Cambridge University Press

Sayre-McCord, Geoff. 2015. "Moral Realism." In *The Stanford Encyclopedia of Philosophy*, edited by Edward N. Zalta. https://plato.stanford.edu/entries/moral-realism/.

Sayre-McCord, Geoff. 2012. "Metaethics." In *The Stanford Encyclopedia of Philosophy*, edited by Edward N. Zalta. https://plato.stanford.edu/entries/metaethics/.

Sayre-McCord, Geoff. 1986. "The many moral realisms." In *Southern Journal of Philosophy* (Supplementary Volume), 24, p. 1–22.

Schueler, G.F. 1988. "Modus Ponens and Moral Realism," In *Ethics* 98, p. 492-500.

Smith, Michael. 1994. "The Moral Problem." Oxford: Blackwell Publishers, p. 12f.

Van Roojen, Mark. 2013. "Moral Cognitivism vs. Non-Cognitivism." In *The Stanford Encyclopedia of Philosophy*, edited by Edward N. Zalta. https://plato.stanford.edu/entries/moral-cognitivism/.

Wong, David B. 2008. "Constructing Normative Objectivity in Ethics." In *Social Philosophy and Policy*, p. 237–266.

YOUR KNOWLEDGE HAS VALUE

- We will publish your bachelor's and master's thesis, essays and papers

- Your own eBook and book - sold worldwide in all relevant shops

- Earn money with each sale

Upload your text at www.GRIN.com
and publish for free